NomosBooks
A division of
NomosEntprises, LLC
PO Box 50871
Henderson, Nv 89016
pronextdoor@gmail.com
702-277-0864

The NomosBooks. edition contains the following Library of Congress Cataloging in Publication Data:

By Author and Life-Style Design Coach, Jerry R. Smith,
The 1-Minute Mentoring Relationship: Volume I: "The 100 Way",
Mentored By Black Millionaires
E-Z & Simple Budget Workbook, co-author C. Chanel Smith-Cavaletti
Your S.E.E. Level, a Personal Growth Process
Formula 7, The 7 EZ & Simple Steps to finding solutions
The 12-Phase Workbook
First NomosBooks Trade Printing: January 2008

Table of Contents

Though multi-purpose, this particular workbook is for the military personnel transitioning out of any branch into civilian life. Designed in a way to help first-generation professionals of all ages. Starting with the school-age youth who has decided to become a professional but does not have access to people from the professional world. Secondly, the college-age student who is in college but is challenged in deciding what to major in. Thirdly, for the employee who is looking for source material to be ready for an upcoming promotional opportunity. Having personally gone through all of the before mentioned phases/stages of a career, I know how exciting and rewarding it can be when you are the first in your immediate family with professional ambitions. Any edge you can get to add to your readiness is a big plus. I believe the workbooks simplicity lends itself to the broadest range of career levels and applications.

I am the first in the family to reach my education and professional level. As I look back on both careers—military 1974 -1981, then onto retirement from law enforcement from the Las Vegas Metro Police Department as a Corrections Officer, 1985 -2006 —I can see how differently both of those outcomes would have been had I employed what this exercise offers.

While researching context for the concept, I noticed that many of the people I talked to did not analyze the work-world the way I do here. It is not by any means completely comprehensive—in that it will cover everything you need to know to make your career the best work-life possible—though I do consider this as one of many literary pieces you will need for reference material throughout your work-life.

The concept, "*Careers G.P.S.* for Exploring The Professional Universe," is broken into 6 parts:
> (1)*The Industry, (2) Industry People, (3) Industry Community,*
> *(4) Industry Education/Training, (5)Industry System, all integrated to become*
> *(6) The Professional World.*

As you research or think back on jobs you've had, you should recognize how valuable this approach can be. The exercise is not difficult, but is very powerful.

The parts that are challenging to infiltrate when you bring the concepts to the real world are the *Industry People and Industry Community*. They don't always let you in to be a part of either one or both worlds. The groups you can join depends on how skilled you are in people relationships. It is like playing a game that you are very proficient at. You probably won't play with armatures when you don't have too.

For me, the most abstract of the parts is the *Industry System*. Though I explain it as three simple components, it is more than that when you take it outside of the industry you are working in. The other parts are pretty straight forward.

Well, good luck on your journey to your new-life opportunities, may they be filled with richness, success and stability.

Exploring The Professional Universe©
The six minute exercise and assessment

This GPS workbook is for the person who has decided on a new profession and is looking for directions. It is a sophisticated approach to career planning, management and goal setting. When done properly, you gain insight, awareness, understanding and mastery. A simple but powerful assessment to show you where you are at this point in time. This is also an effective exercise to show you how to get to where you want to go. When you complete the workbook, come back here and be amazed at how much you will grow.

Start by inserting your chosen profession on each line below; then, go to notes and one at a time, go through all six to complete the phrases with thoughts, questions or comments based on what you now know. Think for about a minute on each phrase. Later in the workbook you will expand the time spent on each element.

1. _____ , The **Industry**

2. _____ ,The **Industry People**

3 _____ ,The **Industry Community**

4, _____ ,The **Industry Education /Training**

5. _____ ,The **Industry System**

6. _____ ,The **Professional World**

NOTES

1. **Industry:** <u>What do you know about the industry's history, present and future?</u> _____
_____
_____

2. **Industry People :** <u>What do you know about anyone in the industry?</u> _____
_____
_____

3. **Industry Community:** <u>Do you know where to go to meet people in the industry?</u> _____
_____
_____

4. **Industry Education/Training:** <u>What kind of training is needed to work in the industry?</u> _____
_____
_____

5. **Industry System:** <u>How do the think the industry work as a system?</u> _____
_____
_____

6. **Professional World:** <u>This is where it all comes together, how does it integrate?</u> _____
_____
_____

To get maximum benefit and for more in depth thinking, use *The Formula 7* system in back of book.

Exploring The Professional Universe©

About the Professional World

Notes

Summarize from the exercise, what you learned or otherwise realized

What you know, don't know or would like to know

About the Professional World

_____

_____

_____

_____

_____

_____

_____

_____

_____

_____

_____

_____

_____

_____

_____

_____

_____

_____

_____

_____

_____

_____

_____

To stand on a good foundation, build on the industry's history. Then look at the present status, based on industry standards. You want to know whether the industry and your company are still viable. Lastly, looking at the future, is your industry going to last? Once you determine that it is a good industry, you want to ask yourself where are you going to work? There are four positions you can land: (1) Primary, the raw material stage; (2) Secondary area, the manufacturing process stage; (3) Tertiary, the sales stage; (4) Quaternary, servicing stage. Before you get too far in the career, figure out where you fit! This will help you to decide what to do next. Let that information guide your career path. If you know a person in the industry, ask them for an assessment. If you don't know anyone, research, research, research!

Insert the profession on the line below to complete the phrase. Focus your thoughts, questions or comments for about a minute, all day, or a whole week if you want. *"Industry."* Enter

1._____,*The Industry*

Research and answer:

History of the industry: Why was there a need for this industry? _____

_____

Present status of the industry: What is going on now? _____

_____

Future of the industry: What is the forecast? _____

_____

What area do you want to work in?

Primary—where the raw material or ideas comes from _____

_____

Secondary— manufacturing sector _____

_____

Tertiary— sales sector _____

_____

Quaternary—service sector _____

_____

_____

_____

_____

_____

_____

_____

_____

Notes

Summarize from the exercise,
what you learned or
otherwise realized

What you know,
don't know or
would like to know

<u>*About the Industry*</u>

_____

_____

_____

_____

_____

_____

_____

_____

_____

_____

_____

_____

_____

_____

_____

_____

_____

_____

_____

_____

_____

_____

_____

_____

Now it is time to do some research on people. You are looking for models of excellence and industry leaders. The best thing, however, would be to talk to someone face-to-face. But if you can't, just do the research. Write down what you find, noting things you like about them, and what you want to adopt as your approach to the profession. Get to know industry people.

Insert the profession on the line to complete the phrase. Then in the notes area, write your thoughts, questions or comments from what you found in books, articles, stories or anything online. Think for a minute, all day, or a whole week or more if you want, on *"Industry People."*

2._____,*The Industry People*

Notes

Industry People research
> **Looking for examples of models of excellence**
> **Looking for industry leaders**
> **Site resources**

_____

_____

_____

_____

_____

_____

_____

_____

_____

_____

_____

_____

_____

_____

_____

_____

_____

_____

_____

_____

_____

Notes

*Summarize from the exercise,
what you learned or
otherwise realized*

*What you know,
don't know or
would like to know*

About the Industry People

_____

_____

_____

_____

_____

_____

_____

_____

_____

_____

_____

_____

_____

_____

_____

_____

_____

_____

_____

_____

_____

_____

_____

_____

Some professions have local unions, associations and/or professional organizations that meet on a regular basis. If you can attend a meeting, go! This is where networking goes on, ideas are exchanged and where you can find out more of what is going on in the work place among other things.

Insert the profession on the line below to complete the phrase with thoughts, questions or comments, think for one minute, all day, or a whole week if you want, on the *"Industry Commu-*

3. _____, *The Industry Community*

Notes:

Industry Community activities through
 Professional Organizations
 Unions
 Professional Associations
 Conferences
 Conventions
 Meeting
 Workshops
 other

_____
_____
_____
_____
_____
_____
_____
_____
_____
_____
_____
_____
_____
_____
_____
_____
_____
_____

Notes

*Summarize from the exercise,
what you learned or
otherwise realized*

*What you know,
don't know or
would like to know*

About the Industry Community

_____

_____

_____

_____

_____

_____

_____

_____

_____

_____

_____

_____

_____

_____

_____

_____

_____

_____

_____

_____

_____

_____

_____

_____

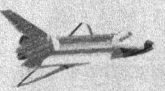

Here you want to know what is involved in qualifying to be called a professional in your chosen field. Do you have the aptitude? What are the curriculums for training and how long are they? This will help you to get ready to excel earlier than most. Always look to upgrade your skills.

Insert the profession on the line below to complete the phrase. Focus on your thoughts, questions or comments for about a minute, all day, or a whole week if you want on *"Education/ Training."* Enter notes below.

4._____,*The Industry Education/Training*

Notes

Industry Education/Training research
> **Vocational school**
> **Jr. Colleges**
> **University level**
> **Specialized training**
> **Online courses**

_____

_____

_____

_____

_____

_____

_____

_____

_____

_____

_____

_____

_____

_____

_____

_____

_____

_____

About the Industry Education/Training

Notes

Summarize from the exercise,
what you learned or
otherwise realized

What you know,
don't know or
would like to know

About the Industry Education/Training

_____

_____

_____

_____

_____

_____

_____

_____

_____

_____

_____

_____

_____

_____

_____

_____

_____

_____

_____

_____

_____

_____

_____

_____

The catch phrase is "know the system." The simplest way we look at "this system" is: you, the product or service you provide, the customers/clients and the relationship between the three organized for a common outcome. When you get that, you are better than most in mastering your field. The person equipped with this knowledge has begun to know secrets only known to a small number of highly successful people.

Insert the profession on the line below to complete the phrase. Research and focus on your thoughts, questions or comments for about a minute, all day, or a whole week if you want on

5. _____ , *The Industry System*

Notes

Industry System research:
What is the relationship between you, your product/service and your customers/clients?

_____

_____

_____

_____

_____

_____

_____

_____

_____

_____

_____

_____

_____

_____

_____

_____

_____

_____

_____

_____

_____

About the Industry System

Notes

Summarize from the exercise,
what you learned or
otherwise realized

What you know,
don't know or
would like to know

About the Industry System

_____

_____

_____

_____

_____

_____

_____

_____

_____

_____

_____

_____

_____

_____

_____

_____

_____

_____

_____

_____

_____

_____

_____

_____

Look for help with this step...hint, mentor. You want to integrate all of your findings together to figure out what you have. A summary of the other five parts are added here to complete the big picture. Very few people do this type of exercise for their career planning. This is only a small part of what it takes to become a successful professional, but it is a good place to start. Good luck!

Insert the profession on the line below to complete the phrase. This is what makes up the "Professional World." Enter notes below.

6. _____ *The Professional World*

Notes

Discuss how all of the elements integrate to make up the professional world in this space.

_____

_____

_____

_____

_____

_____

_____

_____

_____

_____

_____

_____

_____

_____

_____

_____

_____

_____

_____

_____

_____

_____

_____

_____

_____

Notes

Summarize from the exercise,
what you learned or
otherwise realized

What you know,
don't know or
would like to know

About the Professional World

_____

_____

_____

_____

_____

_____

_____

_____

_____

_____

_____

_____

_____

_____

_____

_____

_____

_____

_____

_____

_____

_____

_____

_____

_____

_____

_____

Formula 7 Worksheet
Using Formula 7's EZ & Simple Steps

**This process will help you with problem solving and decision making.
Take each element, one at a time, and go through all 7 steps below.**

1. Start, only start, a list of 100 things you know, don't know, like to know about

_____

_____

2. Search for answers (Cite the source).

_____

_____

3. From what you found out, what can you do now or later?

_____

_____

4. Schedule when you want to start (Copy to calendar, day planner).

_____

_____

5. Action steps to take.

_____

_____

6. Track, evaluate, make changes, adjust.

_____

_____

7. Repeat process with the next item on the list of 100

_____

_____

Schedule next session_____

_____

What are your action Steps_____

_____

Notes

The space below is to write a brief summary on each element's result :

1. Industry _____

_____

2. Industry People _____

_____

3. Industry Community _____

_____

4. Industry Education/Training _____

_____

5 Industry System _____

_____

6. Professional World _____

_____

The Strategic Plan

Use results from the summary above to make plans. Look for a mentor to help out here!

_____
_____
_____
_____
_____
_____
_____
_____
_____
_____
_____
_____
_____
_____
_____
_____
_____
_____
_____
_____

Notes

Notes

Notes

Notes

Notes

Notes

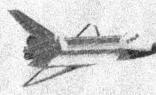

Notes

Notes

Notes

Notes

Notes